Integration

Integration:

(shadows, acceptance and catharsis)

A Primer to Creation

Dustin Cunningham

*

I am grateful for this day
This opportunity
This opportunity to live love and learn
I am great full for all my experiences
My experiences hold no value
Except the value I place on them
I label my experiences as divine
Simply another part
I am of the perfection of the universe
Every star has its place
I have a place
I have a purpose
That place is me and that purpose is to be
I fulfill that purpose with ease and grace
Everyday
I am the wheel
I am the day
I am the power
I am the love
There is no power greater than me

*

I saw something
Looking deep in your eye
Past the facade
I saw a lie
I shouldn't have let it go
But the butterflies
The rush of blood
I understand
I thought
I could
Stop it
I understood
My need too
Perfect
Hiding inside the lies
I always wondered
What you thought
About my eyes
Did you see me decide

*

There is always a choice

*

Awareness
It's getting bigger
What if it's too much
It always has
Will it be
It is
Brain shutting down
Feeling fear
As I run away
Feel the shame
As I stay
I don't know what to say
Please come back
Don't be afraid
But the world won't see me
I'll take all the blame
Mine or not
I am crushed the same
From all the pain
I didn't even make
You have always told me
That's my job
How to be a man
Stand up and take it
Bend over
Let yourself be raped
Having a dick is enough
For you to judge who I am
I was taught how wrong
I didn't ever belong
Such a shameful thing
You cut part of it off
Threw my parts in the trash
You taught me
I was better broken
Severed
Shamed

And in pain
Sitting alone
I've learned more of the same
Your words
Don't match your deeds
I have watched you lie
Over and over
I hope it stops when I die
Find some wings
Instead of running
Maybe it will be time to fly
Just let go of the pain
Find peace and love
As I float in the sky

*

Finding my way home
Back to myself
The authentic self
What is home
How do I know I'm there
Is it terror and fear
Blame and shame
Lies manipulation and pain
The only home I've ever known
That's a problem you see
Because that's what my home
Put into me
When I look for a home
I keep finding the same
I look at the world
And really want to join
I see all the joy
All the fun
How bright it is in the sun
I tell myself to join
That world was meant for me
Take of my armor so everyone can see
Me
I know I'm not enough
That's all that is seen
I hear the words
Feel the air
Sit in it again
It feels like home
And I don't want to be here

*

My vision changed
Eyes the same
Filter replaced
Not seeing shame
Power found
In the way

*

I want to run away
Run away from home
I can't run away from me
My authentic self
What do you mean
Who the fuck am I
If not me
I can't take away…
The scars and stars
They are all a part of me
Who could I have been
A different life
Circumstances and challenges
Who could I be
Doesn't matter
Wouldn't be me
I authentically am
Who I am
Because of what I've seen
Theres no going back
And no, I won't stay
Maybe the way
Is to start building a new Dustin today
So my intention is clear
I am only building
No removing
Dismantling
Destroying
All of me will be used
Because all of me is good
I will examen
rearrange
And add
I will learn to love me
I will grow stronger
I will make me
What I want to be

In a word
Maybe it's free

*

Gazing across the way
Trying to not look to hard
Really just not wanting to be seen
Looking
The way
You moved your hand
But it was
Hard
I watched you breath
Faster
I saw you close your eyes
And a tremble
Your breasts rise and fall
How soft you feel
In my hand
And when you leaned back
Fantasy maybe
But I needed
A taste
No not this soon
I don't want to wake
One more moment
Squeezing
As I pushed closer
That last deep breath
And both a release

*

Thank you for the gift
The lesson I learned
You taught me
How you treated me
How you allowed me to be treated
How you allowed yourself to be treated
You did it for me
I learned that I couldn't
You watched me abused
I learned I wasn't worth protecting
I watched you abused
Learned it was okay
Left alone
With my immature brain
Learning only what I had
Left alone
With only what I knew
What I know
Smash my face against
Making holes in the wall
Trying to find something new
Left alone
Only what I knew
But I had my present
That I got from you
So shiny and pleasant
Expensive and hard to find
Left all alone
Except for
My present
And some monsters in my mind

*

Don’t say a word
I’ve learned enough
The way you move your
Beautifull hips
Tell me all I need to know
Except I’m still deciding
If I should lift, you up
Or hold you down
My perfect prize
I’ve won the night
My celebration song
The moans you can’t deny
My good little girl
Look me right in the eye
It’s lust and love
While I’m deep inside
It’s okay if you cry
Smothered in my embrace
Gentle with your heart
But ravenous with your taste
My beautiful queen
Deep inside you are seen

*

Healing the wounds
Left on a boy
Left by his mother
In a world that says
Happy wife happy life
And hides all the lies
If you think I love you
Your probably wrong
Probably the same
You just hide the shame
Look for the darkest
Place it will fit
Caution my dear
We make our own
Light in here

*

I wanted to write you a letter. So many really, what words to say? How much I tried and failed. Tried to hold on so tight, hurt my hands. Held my breath and tried to breath. I clenched my jaw and broke my teeth. Ask you for forgiveness for all my mistakes. Yelled when I should have cried. Wishing I could have lied. When I lost you. Wishing I had died. Wanting to just run and hide.

Tell you I love you as much as I could. If there was anything I could see, I would. Begged and pleaded. Went all the way. Kapt being defeated. Never gave up. Even though I tried. Looked for an opening, an opportunity, a choice. Doubled down. Bet everything, I had. Lost every time. Spent every last dime. So, I could tell you I love you and hold you one more time.

Made friends with the demons and gods. Magic and prayers. Just kept asking why. How do I undo all the things that took me from you? Is there anyone who could help me back to you? When could I hold you again? And cried and cried, when I still couldn't see the way. Maybe someday, but I know not today. Resigned to a fate because I didn't say no.

How I miss you playing in the snow. Not in my worst nightmares, did I think you would be gone in a blink. I'll try to keep holding myself together. So afraid this pain will last forever. But honestly, I don't know how much more I can bear. If there's one chance. And there is. I'll be there still there. Looking for the words for what I want to say to you. I'm sorry my babies and I love you.

Dad

*

To Answer:

Maybe I should sit down
Spend a little time to think
And what about that question
Coparenting
Never has it happened not even for a blink
For the longest time I figured
It was my stubbornness and pride
Deep down from this newfound view
I actually discovered something new
I was rather compliant and offered much grace
Maybe it was more of a problem
I offered it while she lied to my face
Parallel parenting was the best we could achieve
Because Ann could not overcome her compulsion
To deceive
I don't think that's what she really wanted
And I do think she tried
I think when she was a kid
Too much trauma got buried deep inside
It hurt her so much
It could never get out
Today living with all that pain
All she can do is scream and shout
From my desire to help all around
Silent compliance the biggest mistake I've found
Except the occasions I saw my child bleed
A thunderous roar as my heart would pound
My desire to protect so deep so strong
In my DNA and supported by society all along
Until of course
That desire is to protect something from you
Something you so desperately want to keep out of view
So, for the most part quietly
I sat
Afraid to do something new

I felt your vengeance many times before
When the light started shining
On something you wanted to hide
Regretfully complied
Until that day our child started threatening suicide
Nothing can stop what I'm going to do next
Hang the fuck on
You're coming along for this ride
I've seen all the shadows
And felt the damage done
Right now I'm grabbing them
And heading straight for the sun

*

Thanks for understanding
I heard what you said
I know what you meant
It was little child you
Hurt
Scared
Really needing to vent
Thanks for understanding
The more you act out
The more I learn
Why I am here
And what to do on my turn
Thanks for understanding
I am the balance that simply must exist
I am the light and love
That your darkness simply must resist
Thanks for understanding
Resist isn't my job in this game that we play
My job is to flow
Thank you for teaching me what I needed to know
Thanks for understanding
I am the faith
In something I don't think you can see
The faith in the perfection of all of us
You
And me
Thanks for understanding
I am the sparkle of light where darkness reigns
I am a lover, a fighter, and a healer of pains
Thanks for understanding
In the worst of times
You hear them calling my name
Medic, they once called me and they will once again
Thanks for understanding
I know you won't like some of the things I must do
But nothing will stop me
From bringing all of the medicine to you

Thanks for understanding
I understand deeply
Some we will lose
I understand deeply
My job is to do what I can
I understand deeply
I must take a stand
Thanks for understanding

*

Saw the message from you
Found that I was immediately aroused
Thoughts of your voice
Your smile
That touch
The one that needed to wait
I can until the time is right
Maybe tonight
I don't think its fate
Just the choices we make
What choices indeed
Would bring you to me
For the application of our hearts
With some safety of course
But that's not really the point of love
Love isn't always safe
Controlled
Or predictable
Its much more like the stars up above
It happens when it does
Often without reason or rhyme
Waiting so hard
Kind of sick of this thing they call time
You and me
Would it be OK if I told you my dream
All the ways I would like to make you scream
Maybe I should say
Will someday
Saying don't stop
Begging for more
If I try hard enough
I already hear you knocking on my door
I know what you will do to me
And somewhere I'm sure I'm ready to see
I might moan and accidentally say no
Please my beauty
Don't listen

Don't let go
Dimly of course
But the lights stay on
Because in my dream I can seed
Exactly what you beautiful body looks like
On top of me
Something I'm missing
Keep waking before I get to
That's how this exchange ends
I think it's best
I leave that part up to you

*

Universal download 1/6/25 174HZ

It is what I will
A certain amount of movement is necessary
Don't ask me if you're not ready
I am
What else can I be
I know
I will not
Hold on
It's okay
I love you Dustin
Another part died
Perfectly displayed
No other way
Conflicted between you two
Can I push them together
It does what it does
Maybe must
Challenge
And I do
I am the voice that won't go away
I will
I will not
Eternal
The sea
The fire
The sky
I feel you shaking
I see you cry
The voice that won't go away
The darkness
The day
The pleasure
The pain
The words once again

The words once again
Word
Speak
And I will
Hard work to find
Something divine
Nothing Is real
Something
Floating away
Make it stop
I won't even if I could
And I could
All
You said
You wanted
And I will
What do you need
I know
Expression I must
Run
What did you say
Run deeper I go
Defi
Lie
I do them for you
Find
Me
That's all there is
Defi
Was above no bellow
Fuck
It's all inside of me
See
I do
New
Right on the edge
Extend
Again

Die inside
End
No
Again
Extend
That was a lot we brought up
Rest friend

*

I watched your panties getting wet
While you said you were afraid
Can’t quiet figure out what it is I might have said
Pretty little pink thongs and polka dots dancing along
Fuck you I said it, I can pretend to be strong

*

I heard there was a word
A secret mystical one I never learned
People kept saying it
I kept asking what did it mean
Floating there just out of my grasp something like a dream
Often so angry because I heard it was everywhere
Apparently blind, it's something I couldn't see
Fortunate this time to be a stubborn as me
Someone pointe and told me it was in my own hand
Not bellow, not above
Been looking sense day one, and this thing is called love
It makes sense inside of me, would be the last place I look
What I felt inside
And when I showed people, they trembled and shook
The cycle of fear
Inward and out
Seem to be the only thing I could hear
I had been looking for something, someone to take that away
Do away with all the hate and take away the grey
Some did try
But never did stay
Really just cover it up when I wanted to hide
None of it ever gave me what I needed inside
When I did find it, and could finally see
That thing I needed was always inside of me
Anger again for a life I felt was a waste
Sat with it once again
What a miraculous taste
Hard as can be, and really that's what it was
Gave me all the strength I needed to rise above
Hard as can be, learning to be me
So much beauty, I found, learning to be me
And what do I do now that I know
Love is a must, but who should I show
Of course, once again, in the palm of my hand
Radically loving myself in this violent land
Loving myself, so proud and so strong

Freely giving myself what I needed all along
Mountains singing in their thunderous voice
This is my time, this is my choice
No regret for the choices I made to get here
Taking in all the lessons, still ringing in my ear
Excepting it all so deep and so wide
The only rule, love everything inside
The deeper I go
The more that I know
The more I see
The more I am free
The more I am happy
When I choose to be me
And something else that I found inside
There is no longer any reason for me to hide
Now I must go, to show what I know
Balanced and confidant in my way
Owning my light and darkness today
Nothing greater
Nothing can compete
No chance of defeat
I am the one source
One power
One love
Perfect and whole
Integration complete

*

I feel it drawing near
Good information in the fear
The story of scars unseen
Of the ones who said they loved
And placed their needs above
It's the best I can do
Bleed my pain onto you
Love you I tried
Maybe you did
I almost died
That's why I ran away
Never felt safe enough to play
I brought my shame
Found much more of the same
Made kids of my own
Lived in a masterfully broken home
Even sitting right there
They were always alone
Thought if I stayed, I could
I could hold it together
Kept moving closer to never
Speaking the truth silenced
More violence
Where is my voice
Where is my choice
Where is the love you said
Just fuck me in bed
Fucking with my head
So hard to see through
So hard to see you
So hard to see what is was
Abuse
Fuck look what I said
And actually
If feel better outside my head
I didn't know that I could
Wasn't sure I would

Look what I did, it was me
Teaching myself to be free
Fear that once caused me
To run away
Once I looked closer
Was actually strength today

*

I have found a way
To change everything you say
From weakness into power
From work into play
Your words still hurt me, they do
But I have found inside of me strength is created too
I know that your words are not something that define
This strength and this power is mine, divine
Your weakness and fear
Have no power here
Except I'm sure you will find
To enhance my ability to leave you behind
Move away from the fight
And step into the light
Truth, my friend
The only possible end

*

What a sick feeling
Realizing what you did
What happened
What you convinced me to do
To be
To fill your void
Your self-hate
With my love
My love
Taken violently
Manipulated and coerced
What you did
What you did
What you did
Was rape me
I said what I let happen
Still fucking blaming myself
For your filth
Still covered in your stench
Your putrid crotch
Gaping wide
With the blackness
From your heart
I can still smell you
All over my scars
What a sick feeling
Knowing what you did
To me
You did
To me

*

Thank you for being my friend
For seeing me
For caring
Taking the time
Listening and learning
Breathing with me
Using your beautiful eyes to see
Feeling with your heart
And moving cautiously
Crying and overwhelmed
And an urge to pretend
So afraid a mistake
Will bring it to an end
Started feeling so much
I know what happens
When my brain gets stuck
I need to take my time
Let it move through
Teach it and learn
To do something new
I know where I am
And where I want to go
Eyes open looking
For the best way to grow
I have to start where I stand
Realizing the power I need
Is in my hand
I wish for a map
Leading the way
Tomorrow forever an illusion
Only today
Illuminate this moment
Feeling thought action
Stand in my truth
And own it
Slow down and breathe
It's time to be free

*

I found you in the stars
Marveling at the perfect placement
Where they all are
In out around
Everywhere
Not a mistake to be found
Realized
It's also a universe inside
All that is
Must include me too
It that's where I pray
Maybe I should respond
To the desires I say
Yes
Love is what we make today

*

A weapon
A means to an end
To serve
To a dishonest master
Unsure of the nature
Unaware on the balance
Use us to fill the hole
Of your awareness
Your fear
Inadequacy
To create
Take our hands
To cover on blood
An instrument to you
To sooth
So often what you choose
We build the walls
That keep you safe
Hold you when you shake
Keep the lights on
To hide your shadow
We are your violence
We are your pain
We are your shame
The substance creating
The world you will
You are the space we fill
Do your best to keep us away
From the lies you say
Perpetuate the story
Hiding in your worry
In every little boy
Manipulated like a toy

*

I like it
When I can feel
You are afraid
Reminds me
You are the prey
That primitive piece inside
You
Moan and whimper
Growl and howl
A lot of healing
Teaching and learning
Acceptance of the yearning

*

I like it
When I feel afraid
Might
Scratch and bite
I bet you
Could hurt me just right
Might
Say the right words
To se of the fight
Nothing like that feeling
Of suffering tonight
Better pull my motherfucking hair

*

I need to feel defeated
Mind and body
Torturing my soul
Something to fill the hole
Someone to act out on
Run
What you think it is
Actually
Not fun
I know how to use
To soothe
Feel home in the hate
Fuck fuck
What I want to create
I want to be defeated
Want more fear
Throbbing aroused
I'll find you
Itching clawing inside
Devious ride
It's not that I don't care
Just not about you
Too kind and fine
A type not mine
Too much in line
Need the pain
Right fucking now
If you won't do it
No
I'll make you somehow
Think I'm joking
At three
You'll see
defeated

*

From your asserted state
Dysregulated state
You state
Truth
You
Eye reveals
Egos flee
The mirror of me

*

No means
No
motherfucker

*

How do I want to be touched
Sometimes softly
Like an equal
Like someone is excited to touch me
Like I am beautiful
I want to feel the push coming from both sides
I want to be touched everywhere
Like my whole body matters
My whole body matters
Sometimes firmly
Sometimes I want to get fucked
With love and passion
Sometimes looking me in the eye
Holding me tight
Always spending the night
Like you are going to keep me safe
Like I'm precious
And that's how I want to touch you too

*

My genitals so often don’t feel safe

*

I can make your genitals feel unsafe too

*

I know how it feels
I know how scary it is
To feel those feelings
To want so badly
To control them
To want them to go away
I know how it feels
To see yourself
Acting out
Making them worse
I know how scary it is
Watching yourself
Out of your own control
Creating those things
You want no more of
I know how it feels
Alone
Frightening
Hopeless
Helpless

*

The light was just so bright
All the stars and planets
Aligned
It just felt so right
To leave something unwanted behind
The next day
I just woke up and went on my way
Realized after a while
Something felt off
There was something gone
Honestly it feels kinda wrong
Abandoned a part
That had been there so long
Why the surprise
For as long as I could remember
I was asking it to go away
Because a thousand times over
What it did was stay
With that gone now
Not really knowing what to say
What do I do
Without you
Telling me
I don't matter
There's something I have to prove
Not enough and unworthy too
I have to justify and make it right
Sacrifice what I am
To make it through the night
Ever sense I found them
I've been wishing these words gone
So alone in the silence
Without these echoes of violence
Empty inside
Still wanting to hide
There's nowhere to go
I've tried

I already know
Infinite solutions
Only one seems really clear
It's time for me to put
Something else in here
I've called for this power
From the depths of my soul
For the opportunity
Someone to fill this hole
And when I started praying
Couldn't imagine that someone was me
Couldn't imagine it
Because it was still just a dream to be free
Now that I am from these things stuck inside
I guess it's time to start making me
Probably going to be a bumpy ride
Hold on tight
But no need for fear
The life I want
I can feel is near
Let me say that again
The life that I want
Is finally here

*

In and out so different it would seem
The eyes controlled by egos deceive
So define what's seen
Often called the devil
Lucifer the name
Bringer of light indeed
Shamed
By those still afraid to see
In the darkest hour
Truth I devour
Let the blood drip down my face
Painful it is
Human race
Lies will not avail
Perpetuate the tale
Creating our own hell
I have a different story to tell
Perfect balance
Help you see
Sometimes the medicine hurts
Hatred felt is not me
Painful but works
Observed already free
For some still too heavy a toll
Understanding you have control
Like oden indeed
Pluck out your eye
Blinded only see you
And what you hold true
Welcome to the power
Create something new
Or maybe choose to suffer more
Either way I'll hold open the door

*

I want you for a minimum of two hours
I want you in my bed
I want to be naked the whole time
I want to hold each other and talk first
I want it to be slow
I want lots of foreplay
I want to feel both of us get wet
I want you to touch me everywhere
I want you to find what I like
I want to find what you want
I want to watch your face when I make you cum
I want to make you moan
I want you to make me wait as long as I can
I want you to tell me how you want it
I want to give it to you just like that
I want to hold each other as we catch our breath
I want, if just for a moment, for us both to be free

*

A rage I can't define
Except
Mine
What do I call myself
When you have left
Nothing left
Nothing less
Nothing left
What's inside
Is it still a lie
Rage I hide
Why
Tone shifting in my ear
Fear
I don't want to breathe
Need
Seed
Perpetuate
Hate
Is it fate
Irate
Can't contemplate
Force
Will
Still there
Clenching aching
Taking
No more
Tore
Addicted
Convicted
Still there
Pulling hair
Don't want to breathe
Relieved
Dreams
Still hate

Awake
Feel too much
Never enough
Cry
Coward die
Release me
Free
Never see
Never me
Never be
Rehearsed
Coerced
Be
Hate
Rage
Fate
Don't want to breathe
It still was me
Still
All I see
I can't do it
And I do keep holding onto you
Actually slower
Not better
Just running low
Revel while I can
It'll come again
I'm glad for what I said
Read it again

*

I do know your name it would seem
Yesterday I couldn't quite say
Last night I found it in a dream
Not the nightmares from which I once hid
Call them nightmares
Call them scary
Hide from the information that they carry
Call you silence
Call you science
Pretending to be truth
No better than the religions
You attempt to disprove
I call you process in progress and sitting still
I call you any attempt to dominate human will
I call you god and the devil and human ambition
I call you any challenge to sublime intuition
Morals and ethics and virtues and vices
That repeated story of how good the light is
I call it so bright we cant even see
I call it anyone doing anything that interferes with someone being free
Controls manipulations and advertisements on tv
I call it you sitting there starring
I also call it me
I call it a need
I call it the perfect result of perfect faults
I call it here and now
Somewhere and somehow
I call it right fucking now
Violence and peace
Smiling through broken teeth
You cowards I call it my power
Sit there just fucking holding your flowers
I will call it in my choice
And I will call it in my voice
You may call it obscene
But it will be seen

*

Stand there arms crossed
Pretending your still mad
Still giving me those fuck me eyes
Knowing I'd still take you from behind
Well you've got my address bitch
Bring her too I'll line you up in a row

*

Choose your own adventure
But you don't know that's the game we are playing
I think I'm going to leave you in charge
Go ahead and burn the fucker down

*

I see success

*

Current understanding is fuck you
But just you motherfuckers over there
Was there satire in their
Or was he really fucking serious
Might just be the drugs
And fuck was he talking about you
I'm over here meditating
And you're trying to burn me down

*

Did you find yourself routing for Kong
What was the moment
You realized you were wrong
What was the moment
You saw the good was the dark
Was there a moment
You felt it in your heart

*

More than an escape
Maybe reprieve
Release
The energy perfect to see
Perfect to just be
Feel that line
Separate unique
Connected and whole
The earth under my feet
Although it is
Doesn't feel the same
Somehow less shame
An acceptance and knowing
In the breeze blowing
Letting go
Not clinging to old stories
Victories or glories
Peaceful knowing
It is only what it is
And I am curious to know
Held perfect precise
Infused from within
Water just right
Balance the hot and cold
Just enough pressure
Patience
Let the medicine in
Magical across my skin
Patience
Because deeper too
Found the spot needed
Found also healing in you
Thinking about all the elements
That made tonight
Not visible
To the naked eye
Crucial nonetheless

That fire inside
The power and pressure
Made it all come alive
The heat
Allowing us to thrive
So often denied
Visceral primal animal inside
And that heat
Almost scared for death
Made me feel more alive
Not just that
Feel my will
My ability to thrive
A knowing and trusting
Of who I am
And what I can
Not just me
But we can
Together
Make a moment to just be
To just see
No need to flee
A moment to love
Being free
And that heat
I still feel it right there
Rubbing on my body
Playing with your hair
And element of acceptance and trust
Thrown into the mix
It was magic I couldn't resist
Maybe better said
Magic straight from the heart
I can still feel it right there
That beautiful heart
Like a star shining bright
Illuminating a dark cold night
Just right

A learning
A growing
A healing

*

Still deciding on all the rules of the game we're playing. But this much I will say. All are welcome to the darkness. I will fucking bite you. After that, I do have ice cream if you're inclined to stay. Otherwise fuck off sincerely. Healing through radical acceptance going on here. It was kinda violent tonight, lots of spitting.

*

Don’t make me say it again
I’ll fuck you both at the same time

*

Nope
Not quite done defiling
Myself

*

At the end of the day
We are still animals
Universal rules apply

*

Kundalini says raise the energy from your crotch
I say fuck that my dick creates worlds
and you want me to run from that energy
And hid it in my brain
Never again
My energy is perfect exactly where it is
No shame
Whole perfect and complete
Except for the pieces they cut off of me
Trying to instill the same

*

I went to the creek
I felt like crying
I couldn't get it outcomes
The creek was soothing
I thought it might have helped
Take it away
It didn't
Still there
Started pouring out
As I walked through the door
And I remembered why
It's not safe for me to show that outside
Not for me
Not for a man
To be in pain
So much shame
Because I feel
Yeah fuck the patriarchy
And every one of your feminist friends
Acting exactly the same
For all that pain
Put into me
And every innocent boy you see
Fuck you completely
My hate
Perfect response
to what you make
Vulgar attempts to protect your power
Put it in the children you fucking coward
Fuck silence
Another form of violence
Not yet totally free
From all this pain
But I am ready to let you see
What you created
All the suffering
society fated

I’m ready to feel it
And honestly
Remake it
Fuck your rules
Ignorant repugnant fools

*

Quantum physics supports the statement:

“Fuck your reality! I’m making my own!”

*

One cannot FIGHT for PEACE

*

Scientists are some of the worst zealots
Of our age.

*

I challenge your claim to this domain

*

Your belief is not a requisite

*

It a healer is willing to tell you something is wrong with you, understand the universe is a mirror. All we can do is project ourselves on it. And it will show us what we are. What they are seeing is only themselves.

*

If you pick a man based on his ability to do violence, then what do you think you are going to get?

*

Healing requires time and space. The use of psychedelics allows the individual to negotiate more easily with the value of those terms. Allowing the individual to process at an increased rate.

*

Early enough
Sitting for a moment
Early enough to see coming
To see going
Sit in the moment
Feel it flowing
My resistance not missing
Can't help but feel
Know that something is
Missing
I'm missing
You
Hard to define
I defy
The label is mine
This missing
In me
Is part
In part
Perfection I see
I still can move
Choose
I do
Know some truth
Release attachment
Stories and visions
Of should
Or could
Ego is not a bad word
Despite
It often hurts
Whisper of me
Conjuring to be
Compassionate vision
Plans
Maybe not lifetimes
But lifelines

Imagine infinity
Imagine the odds
Destined to be
Every possibility exists
In the
Words I say
Future I see
In me
Howling
Dancing
Singing
Victory
Already in me
I
Eye
We
It's rising more
Turning again
To reality
I realize
Make real
Complete
Something
New to be seen
Still learning
What words to say
Today
All possibilities within
How could they be
Should
Will
Will be
Is here
And I see
I think
Only me
Endless
Eternal

Flying free
Almost time
But no movement required
Healed
Inspired
Looks like a line
My eyes let me see
Slivers
Just enough
Of the way
Of me
I do have a choice
Destined to be
I sit right here
Tears in my eye
Teaching
Learning
How to cry
Feel it rise
Breathe it in deep
Ground under my feet
Who am I
To defy
Challenge
And stand
Hold it
And let go
My hand
All power within
Smile and frown
Clench and caress
Comfort and kill
Will
Only be me
Only need
Rise
Climax inside
Will need to die

See nothing
Only light
Blinded
Enough to be
What it always was
Is
And will
Be
Perfectly

*

To Leona

You do what you need to do to survive
But don't you fucking pretend to be small
That power
That will inside
Never extinguished
Comfortable in the night
Every choice you make
learning to thrive
lift up your head
Never fucking hide
The beautiful world inside
The ocean in your eyes
Desert breeze in your breath
Fertile and wet as the forest
Sweet grass of the plains in your hair
Stand as the mountains
Unshakable and strong
Nothing else needed
You are perfect all alone
Do what you need my child
But don't you ever pretend to be small

*

We are all separate, or at least it would seem. Our nervous system, solar system, is co-regulating. It seeks a harmonious balance between all elements. Our place is unique of course. Not only in position but in purpose, power, and will. Perhaps it just seems unique. Nonetheless, we do have will, it would seem. At least I do. Because I choose. And when I do, choose, what I choose, also effects you. Given this thought, and knowing what I need, it is easy to see. Exactly how to send the love to everyone in need. The more I love me, exactly me and how I need it to be. My system becomes safe and helps the whole adjust to my new reality. Actually ours, harmoniously. A rising tide raises all ships, true. Separate from the tide, it would seem. Tricky moon indeed. I get to choose, and I do. I choose perfection, and it would seem, I also choose that for you.
I suppose it will take time for the system to adjust. My actions make waves of trust. You will feel me getting better wherever you are, and do your part, and take that feeling of acceptance, into your heart. And then funny enough, sense that's exactly what I needed, you can give it right back to me. A caveat for my ego to hear, everything is included, it always is, some of it will not be pleasant, may feel like hate, they are healed as well. That's where it's needed the most, it would seem. Call them a cunt, if you need, but they are coming along. So then, when I feel something that hurts. The best response is going to be, how do I best love this thing that hurts. I also know that part is connected to me. If I send out hate and fear, that's also what I receive. And that's definitely not what I need. All pronouns are interchangeable it's all the same.

*

Hope is wishing for the best
Faith is knowing the best
Fear is faith in the opposite

*

To anyone out there shaming their ego
You are using it wrong

*

The word “you” such a funny business
Such a bold assumption
That “you should be different from “me”

*

And the realization
I was only ever talking to me

Published by Dustin Makes LLC

Colorado Springs, CO, USA

Dustincunningham.art

ISBN: 979-8-9929442-1-1

LCCN: 2025914414

www.ingramcontent.com/pod-product-compliance
Lightning Source LLC
LaVergne TN
LVHW022017200926
848481LV00007B/2442
* 9 7 9 8 9 9 2 9 4 4 2 1 1 *